CLAUDE MONET

PEPIN®

GIFT & CREATIVE PAPERS

VOLUME

English

Claude Monet

Impressionism is an art movement that flourished primarily in France during the late 19th and early 20th centuries. A characteristic of the impressionist style of painting is that artists sought to depict scenes and objects by capturing reflected light in bold brush strokes and dabs of colour, rather than a lifelike image of the subject itself. Impressionist paintings would not be defined by clear outlines, but by visually oscillating applications of colour representing the natural light emitted.

Claude Monet (1840–1926) is considered the doyen of the Impressionist movement. From his early career, Monet was interested in less conventional ways of treating light in painting, but it was in the late 1860s that he fine-tuned his way of interpreting light with short strokes in dazzling colour schemes. His 1872 painting of the harbour of Le Havre – *Impression, Sunrise* – is considered a defining work, both in the emergence of the style and in the use of the term 'impression'.

In the 1890s, Monet bought a piece of land across the road from his house in Giverny, Normandy and created a pastoral garden with a large lily pond that served as a source of inspiration for hundreds of paintings created over a period of around 30 years. Typical of the many water-lily paintings that Monet created in Giverny is the dream-like atmosphere in which plants, water, shadows and reflected clouds seem suspended in mesmerizing spatial compositions.

Français

Claude Monet

L'Impressionnisme est un mouvement artistique qui s'est développé principalement en France à la fin du XIXe et au début du XXe siècle. L'une des caractéristiques du style de peinture impressionniste est que les artistes cherchaient à représenter des scènes et des objets en capturant les reflets de la lumière par des coups de pinceau audacieux et des touches de couleur, plutôt que de reproduire une image réaliste du sujet en tant que tel. Ainsi, les peintures impressionnistes ne se caractérisaient pas par des contours clairs, mais plutôt par des applications de couleurs oscillant visuellement, afin de représenter la lumière naturelle.

Claude Monet (1840–1926) est considéré comme le doyen du mouvement impressionniste. Dès le début de sa carrière, Monet s'est intéressé aux méthodes moins conventionnelles du traitement de la lumière en peinture, mais ce n'est qu'à la fin des années 1860 qu'il a peaufiné sa façon d'interpréter la lumière par de brefs coups de pinceau et avec des couleurs éclatantes. Sa peinture de 1872 du port du Havre - *Impression, Soleil levant* - est considérée comme une œuvre déterminante, tant dans l'émergence du style que dans l'utilisation du terme « impression ».

Dans les années 1890, Monet achète un terrain en face de sa maison de Giverny, en Normandie, et crée un jardin pastoral avec un grand bassin de nénuphars, source d'inspiration pour des centaines de peintures créées au cours d'une trentaine d'années. Dans les nombreuses peintures de nymphéas que Monet a créées à Giverny, on retrouve l'atmosphère onirique dans laquelle les plantes, l'eau, les ombres et le reflet des nuages semblent suspendus dans des compositions spatiales fascinantes.

Water-Lilies, 1899
Oil on canvas, 66 x 104 cm
Los Angeles County Museum of Art, Los Angeles

Water-Lily Pond, 1917–1926
Oil on canvas, 130.2 × 201.9 cm
The Art Institute of Chicago, Chicago

Poplars at Giverny, Sunrise, 1888
Oil on canvas, 74 x 93 cm
Museum of Modern Art, New York

The Japanese Footbridge, 1899
Oil on canvas, 81.3 x 101.6 cm
The National Gallery of Art, Washington

Spring Flowers, 1864
Oil on canvas, 91 x 116.8 cm
The Cleveland Museum of Art, Cleveland

Water-Lilies, *Nymphéas*, 1906
Oil on canvas, 90 x 93 cm
The Art Institute of Chicago, Chicago

Water-Lilies, 1914–1917
Oil on canvas, 200.7 x 213.3 cm
Toledo Museum of Art, Ohio

Water-Lilies, *Nymphéas*, 1904
Oil on canvas, 89 x 92 cm
The Denver Art Museum, Denver

Deutsch

Claude Monet

Der Impressionismus ist eine Kunstbewegung, die Ende des 19. und Anfang des 20. Jahrhunderts vor allem in Frankreich erblühte. Charakteristisch für den impressionistischen Malereistil ist, dass die Künstler Szenen und Objekte darzustellen suchten, indem sie das reflektierte Licht in groben Pinselzügen und Farbklecksen einfingen, anstatt lebensechte Abbilder des Motivs zu schaffen. So waren impressionistische Gemälde nicht durch klare Umrisse definiert, sondern durch visuell changierende Anwendungen von Farbe, die das natürliche Licht wiedergaben.

Claude Monet (1840–1926) gilt als Altmeister der impressionistischen Bewegung. Er interessierte sich bereits zu Beginn seiner Karriere für weniger konventionelle Arten des Umgangs mit Licht in der Malerei, aber Ende der 1860er Jahre vollendete er seine Art der Interpretation von Licht mit kurzen Pinselstrichen in überwältigenden Farbkonzepten. Sein 1872 entstandenes Gemälde des Hafens von Le Havre – Impression, Sonnenaufgang – gilt als prägendes Werk, sowohl für den aufkommenden Stil als auch für die Verwendung des Begriffs ‚Impression'.

In den 1890er Jahren kaufte Monet ein Stück Land in der Normandie, auf der anderen Straßenseite seines Hauses in Giverny. Dort legte er einen idyllischen Garten mit einem großen Lilienteich an, der eine Quelle der Inspiration für Hunderte von Bildern sein sollte, die er über einen Zeitraum von etwa 30 Jahren malte. Typisch für die vielen Gemälde von Wasserlilien, die Monet in Giverny schuf, ist die traumähnliche Atmosphäre, in der Pflanzen, Wasser, Schatten und reflektierte Wolken in faszinierenden räumlichen Kompositionen zu ruhen scheinen.

Español

Claude Monet

El impresionismo es un movimiento artístico que floreció fundamentalmente en Francia durante el período que abarca finales del siglo XIX y principios del XX. Una característica del estilo pictórico impresionista es que los artistas buscaban representar escenas y objetos a través de la captura de la luz reflejada mediante audaces pinceladas y toques de color, en lugar de representar una imagen realista del propio sujeto. Así, las pinturas impresionistas no se caracterizan por contornos definidos, sino por sus aplicaciones visualmente oscilantes de color que representan la luz natural emitida.

Claude Monet (1840–1926) está considerado como el máximo exponente del movimiento impresionista. Desde los inicios de su carrera, Monet se interesó por los métodos menos convencionales del tratamiento de la luz en la pintura, pero no fue hasta finales de la década de 1860 cuando perfeccionó su método para interpretar la luz con breves pinceladas y una paleta de colores deslumbrantes. Su cuadro pintado en 1872 sobre el puerto de Le Havre –Impresión, Sol Naciente– está considerado como su obra definitoria, tanto en términos del origen del estilo como por el uso del término 'impresión'.

En la década de 1890, Monet compró un terreno enfrente de su casa en Giverny, Normadía, y construyó un jardín bucólico con un gran estanque de lirios que le sirvió como fuente de inspiración para centenares de cuadros creados durante un largo período de 30 años. Muchos de los cuadros de lirios de agua que Monet pintó en Giverny tienen en común la recreación de una atmósfera onírica en la que las plantas, el agua, las sombras y las nubes reflejadas parecen estar suspendidas en composiciones espaciales fascinantes.

The Water-Lilies, Green Reflections, 1915-1926
Oil on canvas, 200 x 850 cm
Musée de l'Orangerie, Paris

Water-Lily Pond with Irises, 1920-1926
Oil on canvas, 200 x 600 cm
Kunsthaus Zürich, Zürich

Water-Lilies, *Agapanthus*, 1916-1926
Oil on canvas, 200 × 426.1 cm
Kimbell Art Museum, Texas

Water-Lily Pond, Evening, 1916-1922
Oil on canvas, 200 x 600 cm
Kunsthaus Zürich, Zürich

Copyright © 2020 Pepin van Roojen

All rights reserved. No part of this book may be reproduced or transmitted in any form or by any means without permission in writing from The Pepin Press BV.

PEPIN®

Pepin® is a trademark of Pepin Holding BV

Published by
The Pepin Press BV
P.O. Box 10349
1001 EH Amsterdam, The Netherlands
mail@pepinpress.com

www.pepinpress.com

Creative Director / Series Editor
Pepin van Roojen

Layout of this volume
Nina Zulian

ISBN 978 94 6009 123 0

This book is produced by The Pepin Press in Amsterdam and Singapore.